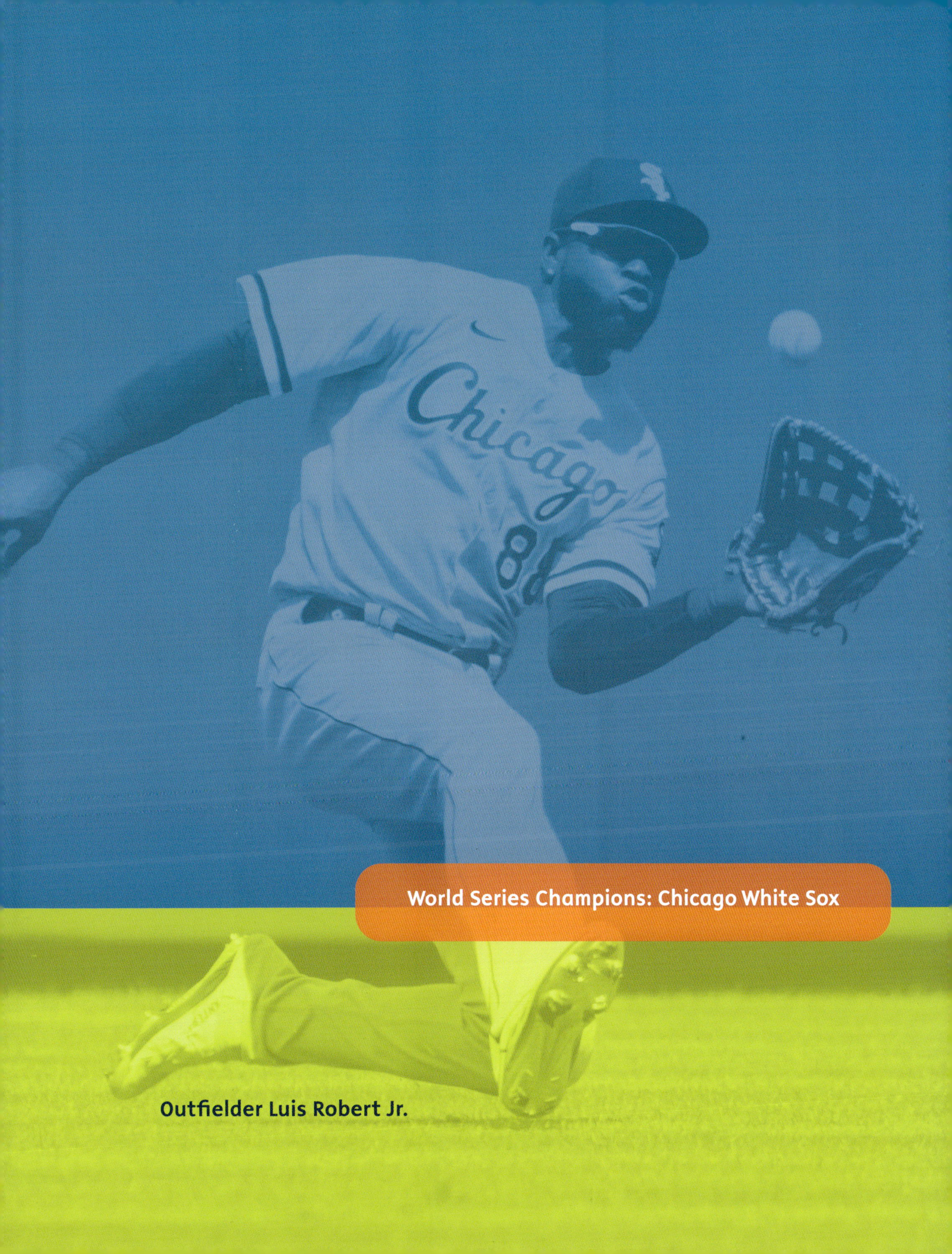

World Series Champions: Chicago White Sox

Outfielder Luis Robert Jr.

First baseman José Abreu

WORLD SERIES CHAMPIONS

CHICAGO WHITE SOX

MEGAN COOLEY PETERSON

CREATIVE SPORTS

CREATIVE EDUCATION / CREATIVE PAPERBACKS

Published by Creative Education and Creative Paperbacks
P.O. Box 227, Mankato, Minnesota 56002
Creative Education and Creative Paperbacks are imprints of
The Creative Company
www.thecreativecompany.us

Art Direction by Tom Morgan
Book production by Ciara Beitlich
Edited by Joe Tischler

Photographs by Alamy (Reuters/Shaun Best), AP Images (Julio Cortez), Getty (Chicago History Museum, Jonathan Daniel, Brace Hemmelgarn, National Baseball Hall of Fame, Michael Reaves, Matthew Stockman, Trancendental Graphics, Ron Vesely, Ed Zurga), Library of Congress, Shutterstock (Sean Pavone)

Library of Congress Cataloging-in-Publication Data
Names: Peterson, Megan Cooley, author.
Title: Chicago White Sox / Megan Cooley Peterson.
Description: Mankato, MN : Creative Education and Creative Paperbacks, [2024] | Series: Creative sports. World Series champions | Includes index. | Audience: Ages 7-10 | Audience: Grades 2-3 | Summary: "Elementary-level text and engaging sports photos highlight the Chicago White Sox's MLB World Series wins and losses, plus sensational players associated with the professional baseball team such as Paul Konerko."-- Provided by publisher.
Identifiers: LCCN 2023008218 (print) | LCCN 2023008219 (ebook) | ISBN 9781640268197 (library binding) | ISBN 9781682773697 (paperback) | ISBN 9781640009899 (pdf)
Subjects: LCSH: Chicago White Sox (Baseball team)--History--Juvenile literature. | World Series (Baseball)--History--Juvenile literature.
Classification: LCC GV875.C58 P47 2024 (print) | LCC GV875.C58 (ebook) | DDC 796.357/640977311--dc23/eng/20230223
LC record available at https://lccn.loc.gov/2023008218
LC ebook record available at https://lccn.loc.gov/2023008219

Printed in China

2005 World Series Champions

Catcher A. J. Pierzynski

CONTENTS

Home of the White Sox

Chicago, Illinois, is a large city along the shores of Lake Michigan. The city is home to the Chicago White Sox baseball team. Fans cheer them on at a **stadium** called Guaranteed Rate Field.

The White Sox are a Major League Baseball (MLB) team. They play in the American League (AL) Central Division. Their **rivals** are the Minnesota Twins and the Chicago Cubs. All MLB teams try to win the World Series to become champions.

Pitcher Ed Walsh

CHICAGO WHITE SOX

Naming the White Sox

The Chicago White Sox were first known as the White Stockings. The name came from the players' white socks. Newspapers had a hard time fitting it into headlines. The team decided on a shorter name in 1904. They became the White Sox. Fans often call the team the "Sox".

Pitcher Doc White

White Sox History

The AL was formed in 1901. The White Sox won the league's first **pennant** that year. They faced the Chicago Cubs in the 1906 World Series. The Cubs had 116 regular season wins. Most people expected them to win. But pitchers Nick Altrock and Doc White kept the Sox in the series. They beat the Cubs in six games and became champions!

The White Sox returned to the World Series in 1917. They beat the New York Giants, 4 games to 2. In 1919, they lost the series to the Cincinnati Reds.

After the loss, the team fell into a **slump** that lasted 40 years. Second baseman Nellie Fox helped the team make the 1959 World Series. But the Sox lost. Hard-hitting outfielder Harold Baines helped the team make the **playoffs** in 1983.

Outfielder Harold Baines

First baseman Paul Konerko

In 2000, the White Sox's luck changed. They started winning more games. First baseman Paul Konerko led the team to the 2005 World Series. They played the Houston Astros. The Sox won the series in four straight games!

Other White Sox Stars

Many stars have played for the club. Fielder Jones managed the White Sox during the team's early seasons. He also played center field. He helped the Sox get to the 1906 World Series. The 1917 championship team was led by outfielder "Shoeless" Joe Jackson.

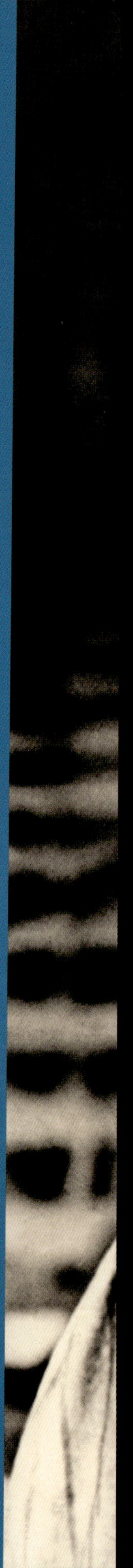

Outfielder "Shoeless" Joe Jackson

First baseman Frank Thomas

The White Sox have had many power hitters. First baseman Frank Thomas played 16 seasons in Chicago. He hit 448 home runs for the Sox. Slugger José Abreu was named 2020 AL Most Valuable Player. He led the Sox to their first playoff appearance in 12 years. Pitcher Dylan Cease and outfielder Luis Robert Jr. hope to keep the wins coming. Is another World Series title around the corner? Fans sure hope so!

About the White Sox

Started playing: 1901

League/division: American League, Central Division

Team colors: black, silver, and white

Home stadium: Guaranteed Rate Field

WORLD SERIES CHAMPIONSHIPS:

1906, 4 games to 2 over Chicago Cubs

1917, 4 games to 2 over New York Giants

2005, 4 games to 0 over Houston Astros

Chicago White Sox website: www.mlb.com/whitesox

Glossary

pennant—a league championship; a team that wins a pennant gets to play in the World Series

playoffs—games that the best teams play after a regular season to see who the champion will be

rival—a team that plays extra hard against another team

slump—a period of time when a team loses more games than it wins

stadium—a building with tiers of seats for spectators

Pitcher Dylan Cease

Index